TABLE OF CONTENTS

Novel-Ties® are printed on recycled paper.

Copyright © 2011, 2013 by LEARNING LINKS

For the Teacher

This reproducible study guide to use in conjunction with the book *Moon Over Manifest* consists of lessons for guided reading. Written in chapter-by-chapter format, the guide contains a synopsis, pre-reading activities, vocabulary and comprehension exercises, as well as extension activities to be used as follow-up to the novel.

In a homogeneous classroom, whole class instruction with one title is appropriate. In a heterogeneous classroom, reading groups should be formed: each group works on a different novel at its reading level. Depending upon the length of time devoted to reading in the classroom, each novel, with its guide and accompanying lessons, may be completed in three to six weeks.

Begin using NOVEL-TIES for reading development by distributing the novel and a folder to each child. Distribute duplicated pages of the study guide for students to place in their folders. After examining the cover and glancing through the book, students can participate in several pre-reading activities. Vocabulary questions should be considered prior to reading a chapter; all other work should be done after the chapter has been read. Comprehension questions can be answered orally or in writing. The classroom teacher should determine the amount of work to be assigned, always keeping in mind that readers must be nurtured and that the ultimate goal is encouraging students' love of reading.

The benefits of using NOVEL-TIES are numerous. Students read good literature in the original, rather than in abridged or edited form. The good reading habits, formed by practice in focusing on interpretive comprehension and literary techniques, will be transferred to the books students read independently. Passive readers become active, avid readers.

SYNOPSIS

Moon Over Manifest juxtaposes two eras: that of the United States in 1918, and that of 1936. Between two world wars, the little town of Manifest, Kansas struggles to deal with the problems of the times,—a shifting demographic, changing views on social class, the impact of a foreign war on Americans, and the growing movement toward unionizing laborers.

When Abilene Tucker's father sends her to live with an old friend in Manifest, Kansas in 1936, Abilene is confused and hurt. She assumes that her father must have some secret reason for parting from her for an entire summer. She must also find a way to fit into a community with secrets of its own. A summer writing assignment from her new teacher, Sister Redempta, challenges Abilene to find a story through which she can define herself and the character of the town she does not yet understand.

Abilene makes her temporary home with Shady Howard, the stand-in preacher and bootlegger who seems to know most of the people in Manifest. But it is the town seer, Miss Sadie, who tells Abilene stories of Manifest during World War I. These narratives feature a cast of characters from the mine bosses to Jinx, a boy who may or may not be someone whom Abilene knows very well. He seems tantalizingly familiar to Abilene. Abilene learns of how the friendship between Jinx and Ned Gillen helped to change the town, and how Shady's protection of Jinx shaped a boy's life.

Abilene makes friends of her own, two girls who join eagerly in a search into the past for a shadowy spy known as "The Rattler." As the three pursue clues to the past, they uncover, if not the Rattler, pieces of the town's history that have survived into the present. Abilene learns of the terrible toll taken by the war and the epidemic of Spanish influenza. She discovers that Ned Gillen did not survive the last months of warfare, and that he was actually Miss Sadie's son, raised with another family in Manifest because of his mother's troubles with the immigration authorities.

Abilene and her friends also discover a series of events that affected the entire town of Manifest. When the Widow Cane died and left behind a substantial tract of land, mine owner Arthur Devlin and his henchmen quickly schemed to lay their hands on the parcel of property that contained a rich vein of iron ore. By a clever scheme of their own, the townspeople, led by Jinx and the commanding Eudora Larkin, succeeded in tricking Devlin into purchasing a less valuable parcel of land and paying off the back taxes so that the town could buy the desirable land.

Finally, the interlocking stories of past and present come together in a climax that heals a wounded community and brings Abilene the fulfillment of her deepest wishes. As summer ends, and with it her visit to Manifest, Abilene sends a heartfelt telegram to her father. The novel ends with Gideon, once known as Jinx, walking toward his daughter and toward a past he could not escape after all.

BACKGROUND INFORMATION

World War I: The Great War

The First World War (1914–1918) took a terrible toll on every nation it touched. Also called The Great War by those who lived through it, this global conflict pitted the Allies (chiefly France, Britain, Russia, and the United States) against the Central Powers (Germany, Austria-Hungary, and Turkey). The seeds of this epic war lay in an intense European nationalism that resulted in the assassination of the Archduke Francis Ferdinand, the heir to the Austro-Hungarian throne, by a Serbian nationalist. A month later, Austria-Hungary declared war on Serbia.

As nations formed alliances based on treaties and enduring sympathies, further declarations speedily led to global war. Germany in particular became an aggressor nation, pitting its forces against the British Navy in a bid to become the dominant European power.

After a period of isolationism, the United States entered the war in 1917, its first troops landing in France under the command of General Pershing. American aid to its allies undoubtedly shortened the war, but casualties among soldiers and civilians were shockingly high, estimated today at 37 million.

The Spanish Influenza

During the war, diseases spread easily because of famine, poverty, and the unsanitary conditions endured by soldiers in the trenches. Spanish influenza became a pandemic from 1918 to 1919, killing more people than bullets or mortar shells. It is estimated that half of American troop casualties in that year-long period were caused by this virulent disease. The Spanish flu, as it was called, was responsible for more deaths than the notorious bubonic plague of fourteenth-century Europe.

The Great Depression

The Great Depression refers to the severe worldwide economic crisis which was precipitated by the Wall Street stock market crash in October 1929. At that time millions of dollars of stock were subject to panic selling in a matter of hours. This forced the closure of many banks whose reserves were involved in stock speculation. Suddenly, the investments of millions of people were lost. In the United States, businesses closed, people lost their homes, and by 1933, sixteen million people, or one-third of the labor force, were unemployed. Complete recovery from the Depression came only with the heavy defense spending for World War II in the 1940s.

Prohibition

The period of Prohibition in United States history was 1920–1933 when the 18th Amendment to the Constitution was in force. The passage of this amendment prohibited the manufacture, transportation, and sale of intoxicating liquors. It represented the culmination of a long campaign by proponents of temperance. This led to bootlegging, or the illegal distribution of liquor, and increased organized crime activity. Public opinion insisted on its repeal by the passage of the 21st Amendment in 1933.

Ku Klux Klan

Often abbreviated KKK and informally known as The Klan, the Ku Klux Klan is the name of three distinct past and present far-right organizations in the United States, which have advocated white supremacy, white nationalism, and anti-immigration, historically expressed through terrorism.

The first Klan flourished in the South in the 1860s, then died out by the early 1870s. Members adopted white costumes: robes, masks, and conical hats, designed to be outlandish and terrifying, and to hide their identities. The second KKK flourished nationwide in the early and mid 1920s, and adopted the same costumes and code words as the first Klan, while introducing cross burnings. The third KKK emerged after World War II and was associated with opposing the civil rights movement and progress among minorities.

PRE-READING ACTIVITIES AND DISCUSSION QUESTIONS

1. Preview the book by reading the title and the author's name and by looking at the illustration on the cover. What do you think the book will be about? Where and when do you think it takes place?

2. Notice the dates that appear at the beginning of chapters in the book from page one to page fifty-seven. Then look at the date that appears on the chapter heading on page fifty-eight. Why do you think the book moves back from 1936 to 1917?

3. War changed the lives of many Americans in the first half of the twentieth century. Read the Background Information on page two of this study guide and do some additional research to learn more about America's role in World War I. As you read this book, notice how war affects the lives of the people of Manifest, Kansas.

4. Read the Background Information on the The Great Depression and Prohibition on pages two and three of this study guide. As you read, notice how the Depression and Prohibition affects the lives of the characters in the book.

5. In this novel, a number of characters keep painful and precious memories locked up inside them. Make a list of the times you kept a powerful memory to yourself. In each case, how did you feel?

6. The author of this novel drew upon the real town of Frontenac, Kansas to create her fictional town of Manifest. If you were to describe the place where you live, what features would you focus on? Make a list of these features.

7. A stereotype is an oversimplified image of a group of people, usually held in common by some part of society. How can stereotypes be harmful? What do you think people can do to overcome stereotyping? Have you noticed any examples of stereotyping in your community or in the media?

8. Grief is an emotion that everyone experiences at some point in their lives. With a group of classmates, discuss how grief might affect us and why the process of grieving is different from all other emotions. Make a list of situations that might cause profound grief. As you read the book, notice how many of these situations occur.

9. In *Moon Over Manifest*, the main character sees life as a puzzle she must solve. What puzzles have you tried to solve in your life? Are there some circumstances that still remain mysterious to you?

10. Notice the cast of characters that appears at the beginning of the book. As you read, refer back to this list in order to keep track of the many characters and place them in the correct story line.

11. Have you read any other books that go back and forth between different time periods? How did the juggling of time sequences affect your understanding of the plot in each of these novels? To keep track of the sequence of events in each of the two time periods in the book—1936 and 1918—list the important events in each era in the order they occurred in the time chart on the following page. The first line of each time chart has been done for you.

Pre-Reading Activities and Discussion Questions

Plot Details

1936	1917–1918
Abilene travels alone to Manifest, Kansas.	Jinx gets off a train and arrives in Manifest, Kansas.

Santa Fe Railway; Hattie Mae's News Auxiliary; Path to Perdition; Shady's Place; First Morning; Sacred Heart of the Holy Redeemer Elementary School; Fort Treeconderoga; Main Street, Manifest; Miss Sadie's Divining Parlor

Vocabulary: Draw a line from each word on the left to its definition on the right. Then use the numbered words to fill in the blanks in the sentences below.

1.	lumbered	a.	period of long ago
2.	vigilant	b.	unwilling; opposed
3.	perdition	c.	run-down; decayed
4.	dilapidated	d.	keenly watchful to detect danger
5.	sparse	e.	puzzling or dangerous situation
6.	antiquity	f.	thinly scattered; scanty
7.	predicament	g.	willing or quick to receive ideas
8.	receptive	h.	moved heavily or awkwardly
9.	reluctant	i.	complete destruction or ruin

. . . .

1. I knew that the class was _____ to my ideas when they applauded my speech.

2. This museum has many statues from _____.

3. The ship's captain was _____ to set sail during the storm.

4. After a summer with little rainfall, the grass was dry and _____.

5. The speaker warned the crowd that bad behavior led to _____.

6. The crew of workers set about repairing the _____ barn.

7. The old grizzly bear _____ through the clearing in the woods.

8. The mother fox was _____ when intruders threatened her offspring.

9. When the bridge was washed away in the storm, many drivers found themselves in a terrible _____.

Santa Fe Railway; Hattie Mae's News Auxiliary; Path to Perdition; Shady's Place; First Morning; Sacred Heart of the Holy Redeemer Elementary School; Fort Treeconderoga; Main Street, Manifest; Miss Sadie's Divining Parlor (cont.)

Read to find out how Abilene settles into the community of Manifest.

Questions:

1. Why was Abilene traveling to a town she had never seen before?

2. What did Abilene mean when she said, "I liked imagining that the chain of that broken compass was long enough to stretch all the way back into his pocket, with him at one end and me at the other"?

3. Why did Abilene jump off the moving train instead of waiting for it to pull into the station?

4. What were Abilene's first impressions of Pastor Howard and his home? What struck her as unusual?

5. How did the actual town of Manifest compare with the town described by Abilene's father?

6. Why did Abilene want to read old editions of the *Manifest Herald* and poke around Shady's living quarters?

7. Why did Abilene think her new life with Shady was luxurious?

8. What did Abilene mean by the term "universals?"

9. Why was Abilene rude to Lettie and Ruthanne when they first visited her at the tree house?

10. Why were the girls frightened by the note left on "Fort Treeconderoga"?

11. Why did Abilene visit Miss Sadie's home? Why did she return after her first frightening visit?

Questions for Discussion:

1. Why do you suppose Gideon sent Abilene to Manifest after she developed an infection from a wound?

2. Why do you think Abilene was fascinated by her daddy's compass that she found in a cigar box?

3. What do you think Hattie Mae was referring to when Abilene overheard her say to Shady, "she needs to know"?

4. Why might Abilene have allowed her classmates to believe that her mother was dead?

Santa Fe Railway; Hattie Mae's News Auxiliary; Path to Perdition; Shady's Place; First Morning; Sacred Heart of the Holy Redeemer Elementary School; Fort Treeconderoga; Main Street, Manifest; Miss Sadie's Divining Parlor (cont.)

5. Why do you think Sister Redempta gave Abilene a summer writing assignment?
6. Do you think Miss Sadie will provide a link to Gideon for Abilene?

Literary Devices:

I. *Simile*—A simile is a figure of speech in which two unlike objects are compared using the words "like" or "as." For example:

> The movement of the train rocked me like a lullaby.

What is being compared?

_____

How does this help you imagine the experience of riding the train?

_____

_____

II. *Metaphor*—A metaphor is a suggested or implied comparison between two objects. For example:

> I've been in and out of schools before, but I'd always been in the protective shade of my daddy. Here I was alone and exposed to the heat and clamor of the day.

What is being compared?

_____

What does this reveal about the role of Gideon in Abilene's life?

_____

_____

Literary Element: Setting
Setting refers to the time and place of the events in a work of literature. What are the two settings in *Moon Over Manifest*?

1._____

2._____

Social Studies Connection:

On page two of this study guide, read the Background Information about the Great Depression and the drought that made economic conditions even worse during the 1930s. Discuss with your classmates conditions that affected the Midwest, where the novel is set.

Santa Fe Railway; Hattie Mae's News Auxiliary; Path to Perdition; Shady's Place; First Morning; Sacred Heart of the Holy Redeemer Elementary School; Fort Treeconderoga; Main Street, Manifest; Miss Sadie's Divining Parlor (cont.)

Language Study: Vernacular

The term vernacular refers to words and phrases that are commonly used in a particular place. Writers often include such language to give the reader an authentic sense of a time and region. For example, Abilene uses words such as *addlepated, doodads,* and *dillydally*; and such phrases as *we got while the getting was good*. Find other examples of vernacular as you read this book and write them down in the chart below.

Examples of Vernacular	Page #	Translation into Standard English

Writing Activities:

1. Imagine that you have just arrived in a town where you do not know anyone. Write a journal entry describing your first day in such a situation.

2. Reread the paragraph at the beginning of the first chapter that describes what Abilene carried with her in a flour sack. Imagine that you are leaving home to stay with relatives or friends for an entire summer. Describe what special things you would take with you in a flour sack, which is about the size of a pillowcase. Explain why each item is important.

Triple Toe Creek; A Bargain is Struck; Likely Suspects; Hattie Mae's News Auxiliary; Miss Sadie's Divining Parlor; The Art of Distraction; Frog Hunting; Miss Sadie's Divining Parlor

Vocabulary: Synonyms are words with similar meanings. Draw a line from each word in column A to its synonym in column B. Then use the words in column A to fill in the blanks in the sentences below.

	A		B
1.	intrigued	a.	anger
2.	concoction	b.	repayment
3.	rile	c.	cheerful
4.	pathetic	d.	praised
5.	restitution	e.	mixture
6.	saunter	f.	joyous
7.	convivial	g.	stroll
8.	touted	h.	fascinated
9.	jubilant	i.	pitiful

. . . .

1. In the early evening, my aunt likes to _____ around her garden, examining the flowerbeds.

2. I knew my cat wanted food when I heard her _____ cries coming from the kitchen.

3. I was _____ by the magician who made his subject seem to float on air.

4. After the war, the nation that had begun the violence had to make _____ to other countries.

5. The advertisement _____ the virtues of a medicine that claimed to cure the common cold.

6. One thing that will definitely _____ our teacher is the failure to turn in assignments on time.

7. The _____ atmosphere of Mrs. Price's home drew many visitors to her door.

8. After our victory on the football field, our coach could only be described as

    _____.

9. When Julie had a cold, her mother brewed her a(n) _____ of tea, honey, and lemon.

Triple Toe Creek; A Bargain is Struck; Likely Suspects; Hattie Mae's News Auxiliary; Miss Sadie's Divining Parlor; The Art of Distraction; Frog Hunting; Miss Sadie's Divining Parlor (cont.)

Read to find out how people from the past come alive in Miss Sadie's stories.

Questions:

1. How did Jinx trick Ned?

2. Why did Arthur Devlin have power over the people of Manifest?

3. Why had the Ku Klux Klan members gathered by Triple Toe Creek? How did Jinx and Ned foil their plans?

4. Why did Miss Sadie say she was a diviner rather than a fortune-teller?

5. Why did Abilene agree to do odd jobs for Miss Sadie?

6. What convinced Abilene that there was truth to Miss Sadie's stories of the past?

7. Where did Jinx live when he came to Manifest in 1917?

8. How did Burton, the pit manager, compel Ned to work a double shift at the mine?

9. Why did Jinx "borrow" a Manchurian Fire Thrower from Mr. Hinkley? Do you think he will return it?

10. What distracted Abilene from further investigation of the grave marker?

Questions for Discussion:

1. Why do you suppose Jinx and his Uncle had parted ways and that Jinx was on the run?

2. What do you think Miss Hattie meant when she said, "The earth speaks loud enough when it wants to be heard"? How might the earth "speak"?

3. What evidence showed that Miss Hattie used her gift of a thesaurus in her article of October 11, 1917? Do you think she used the thesaurus effectively?

4. How do you think Mr. Devlin's policies affected the people of Manifest?

5. What evidence showed that ethnic and racial bias existed in Manifest?

6. Do you think there is a connection between Miss Sadie and Sister Redempta? If so, what might it be?

Triple Toe Creek; A Bargain is Struck; Likely Suspects; Hattie Mae's News Auxiliary; Miss Sadie's Divining Parlor; The Art of Distraction; Frog Hunting; Miss Sadie's Divining Parlor (cont.)

Literary Element:

I. *Point of View*—Point of view in literature refers to the person telling the story. We learn about people and events through this person's eyes. The story may be narrated by a character in the story (first-person narrative) or by the author (third-person narrative).

From whose point of view are the events of 1936 told?

_____

Why do you think the author chose this point of view?

_____

From whose point of view are the events of 1918 told?

_____

Why do you think the author chose this point of view?

_____

II. *Simile*—What is being compared in the following passage:

Memories were like sunshine. They warmed you up and left a pleasant glow, but you couldn't hold them.

_____

Do you think this is a good comparison?

_____

_____

III. *Hyperbole*—Hyperbole means exaggeration for effect. Often, the effect created is humorous. For example, Jinx tells Ned:

What I have here will solve all your problems. It's a cologne, an aftershave, and mouthwash all in one. It comes from the arctic glacial waters off the coast of Alaska. I got it from a hundred-year-old Eskimo medicine man.

Why does Jinx use hyperbole in this passage? How does Ned respond to these claims?

_____

_____

_____

Triple Toe Creek; A Bargain is Struck; Likely Suspects; Hattie Mae's News Auxiliary; Miss Sadie's Divining Parlor; The Art of Distraction; Frog Hunting; Miss Sadie's Divining Parlor (cont.)

Literary Element: Narrative Technique

Writers have different ways of telling a story. One narrative technique, or way of telling a story, is to alter the time sequence. The narrative of *Moon Over Manifest* moves back and forth between 1918 and 1936. What effect does this shifting time sequence have on the plot?

_____

_____

Social Studies Connection:

Do some research to find out about the orphan trains that used to be common in nineteenth and early twentieth-century America. Prepare a brief oral report on the topic.

Writing Activity:

Write about a time when you tried to understand the puzzling behavior of another person or group of people. Tell what you learned from studying the situation.

The Victory Quilt; Pvt. Ned Gillen; Under the Stars; Pvt. Ned Gillen; Hattie Mae's News Auxiliary

Vocabulary: Use the context to help you determine the meaning of the underlined word in each of the following sentences. Then draw a line from each numbered word below to its definition on the right.

- The child <u>grimaced</u> at the taste of the bitter medicine on the spoon.

- Chicken pox is a <u>malady</u> that causes its victims to have rashes and fevers.

- I wanted to write a beautiful song, but I'm afraid my efforts produced <u>mediocre</u> results.

- The <u>raucous</u> cawing of the crows woke me from a deep sleep.

- All that was left of the <u>abandoned</u> mine was a broken down building where the offices had once been.

- Our feelings swung from joy to <u>dismay</u> as we watched the tightrope walker make his way across the wire.

- Since we did not know when you were coming, you will have to accept the <u>haphazard</u> arrangement of furniture in the bedroom.

- On <u>Commencement</u> Day, each student will go up on the stage to receive a diploma.

. . . .

1. grimaced
2. malady
3. mediocre
4. raucous
5. abandoned
6. dismay
7. haphazard
8. commencement

a. characterized by a lack of order
b. terror
c. graduation
d. illness
e. harsh; grating
f. made a facial expression showing discomfort
g. ordinary; barely adequate
h. deserted

> Read to find out whether Jinx launches his business successfully.

The Victory Quilt; Pvt. Ned Gillen; Under the Stars; Pvt. Ned Gillen; Hattie Mae's News Auxiliary (cont.)

Questions:

1. Why were the women of Manifest working on a Victory Quilt in 1917?
2. Why did Mrs. Larkin refuse to associate with Miss Sadie and discourage her daughter from associating with Ned Gillen?
3. What was the source of tension between Ned and Lance Devlin?
4. How had Jinx's Uncle Finn prepared him for the "cons" he perpetrated in Manifest?
5. Why had Jinx come to Manifest "on the run"?
6. Why was an under-age Ned Gillen able to enlist in the army? Why did he want to serve?
7. Why did Jinx place a high bid on the Victory Quilt?
8. What evidence showed that Abilene and her two friends, Lettie and Ruthanne, were superstitious?

Questions for Discussion:

1. How was the town of Manifest divided along class lines in 1917? Is your community divided along class, racial, or ethnic lines? If so, how does this affect you?
2. Do you think Shady imposed a fair punishment on Jinx for selling firecrackers? Was this a better or worse punishment than taking away privileges or using physical force against him?
3. How did Miss Sadie serve as a bridge between the past and the present for Abilene?
4. Do you think the people of Manifest—the young and the old—appreciated the dangers of a world war?

Literary Device: Flashback

A flashback is a scene that takes the narrative back to a time before the current point in the plot. What do you learn about Jinx's life from the flashback that begins on page 124 of the novel?

_____

_____

_____

Social Studies Connection:

Do some research about Prohibition, an era during which alcoholic beverages were outlawed in the United States. How did these laws affect American society? Prepare some notes for a short report to share with your classmates.

The Victory Quilt; Pvt. Ned Gillen; Under the Stars; Pvt. Ned Gillen; Hattie Mae's News Auxiliary (cont.)

Literary Element: Conflict

In a work of literature, a conflict is a struggle between two opposing forces. It may be the struggle of a person against society, a person battling against nature, or a person's inner struggle. Use the chart below to record the conflicts that appear in *Moon Over Manifest*.

Type of Conflict	Examples
Person *vs.* person/society	
Person *vs.* nature	
Person *vs.* self (inner struggle)	

Writing Activities:

1. Write an advertisement for a real or imaginary product in the old-fashioned style of the ad for Velma T.'s Vitamin Revitalizer. Use hyperbole to convince your reader that he or she must buy this product.

2. Write a story with a "beginning, middle, and end" as Lettie suggested to Abilene. Tell about something real or imagined that happened to you.

Miss Sadie's Divining Parlor; Elixir of Life; Hattie Mae's News Auxiliary; Dead or Alive

Vocabulary: Draw a line from each word on the left to its meaning on the right. Then use the numbered words to fill in the blanks in the sentences below.

1. fugitive
2. demise
3. mingled
4. scheme
5. evade
6. abolish
7. peer
8. refuge

a. do away with; stamp out
b. death; termination
c. escape from by trickery
d. person who is fleeing from prosecution
e. mixed; put together in a mixture
f. look searchingly
g. shelter; protection from danger
h. program of action to be followed; plan

· ·

1. If you _____ around the corner, you will see whether the bus is coming.

2. Rather than face a judge in a court of law, the man became a(n) _____.

3. We all ran under the awning to take _____ from the heavy rain.

4. The smell of turkey roasting _____ with the aroma of pies baking in the oven to remind us of wonderful Thanksgiving dinners in the past.

5. It took a serious accident to occur before the town officials agreed to _____ unsafe child labor practices.

6. Some people worry that the growing popularity of "e-books" means the _____ of books as we know them.

7. We were able to stop the jail break from happening once we discovered the prisoners' _____.

8. The film star managed to _____ the photographers by wearing a large hat and sunglasses.

> Read to find out whether Abilene learns about her father's past.

Miss Sadie's Divining Parlor; Elixir of Life; Hattie Mae's News Auxiliary; Dead or Alive (cont.)

Questions:

1. What advantage did Sheriff Dean have over Shady? How did he use his power?

2. Why did Shady protect Jinx from the sheriff? What did he mean when he told Jinx, "I suspect you may have found yourself in the wrong part of the pond a time or two"?

3. What was the significance of the burning wooden cross in front of the German Fraternal Hall?

4. How did Jinx save Shady from the sheriff?

5. Why did Abilene feel frustrated in her search to learn about her father?

6. Why was Abilene walking the tracks in search of specific plants?

Questions for Discussion:

1. Do you think Jinx was justified in tricking the sheriff?

2. In Hattie Mae's News Auxiliary of July 20, 1918, what opinion do you think she held about the attempt to Americanize all things German?

3. What do you think might be the connection between Sister Redempta and Miss Sadie?

4. Why do you think the cork was significant for Abilene?

5. Why do you think Shady wouldn't tell Abilene about her father?

Literary Device: Personification

Personification refers to a figure of speech in which a nonhuman object is granted human characteristics. For example:

> After Ned left, the troubles we had all run away from came
> and found us . . .

What is being personified?

_____

Why is this better than just saying, "our troubles returned"?

_____

_____

Miss Sadie's Divining Parlor; Elixir of Life; Hattie Mae's News Auxiliary; Dead or Alive (cont.)

Science Connection:

Do some research online to find out about the plants Abilene was collecting for Miss Sadie: prickly poppy, skeleton weed, spider wort, and toadflax. Learn about the possible medicinal qualities that are attributed to these plants. Also, find out why spider wort is often planted around nuclear power plants.

Writing Activity:

Imagine that you know all about the life Abilene's father lived in Manifest as a young boy. Write about his boyhood in Manifest and "uncover" a secret that the townspeople may be keeping from Abilene.

Miss Sadie's Divining Parlor; No-Man's Land; Hattie Mae's News Auxiliary; Pvt. Ned Gillen; One Short, One Long; Miss Sadie's Divining Parlor; The Manifest Herald; Pvt. Ned Gillen; Ode to the Rattler

Vocabulary: Read each group of words. Cross out the one that doesn't belong with the others. On the line below the words, tell how the remaining words are alike.

1. fortunate   dismal   gloomy   dreary
    The other words are alike because _____
    _____

2. furtively   cautiously   openly   carefully
    The other words are alike because _____
    _____

3. tampering   supporting   interfering   meddling
    The other words are alike because _____
    _____

4. lively   animated   worried   invigorated
    The other words are alike because _____
    _____

5. impasse   jam   gridlock   release
    The other words are alike because _____
    _____

6. hoax   explanation   subterfuge   trick
    The other words are alike because _____
    _____

7. coaxed   dissuade   cajole   persuade
    The other words are alike because _____
    _____

8. eerie   weird   strange   credible
    The other words are alike because _____
    _____

> Read to find out what happens when the townspeople stand up to the bosses at the mine.

Miss Sadie's Divining Parlor; No-Man's Land; Hattie Mae's News Auxiliary; Pvt. Ned Gillen; One Short, One Long; Miss Sadie's Divining Parlor; The Manifest Herald; Pvt. Ned Gillen; Ode to the Rattler (cont.)

Questions:

1. Why did Abilene continue to work for Miss Sadie long after she had paid off her debt for breaking the pottery?

2. Why did Arthur Devlin have his sights fixed on the property that had belonged to the Widow Cane?

3. Why did Miss Velma's elixir suddenly become popular?

4. How did Miss Sadie's words inspire the townspeople of Manifest to stand up to Arthur Devlin and his crowd?

5. Why was the town of Manifest put on quarantine in the summer of 1918?

6. How did Jinx plan to raise the thousand dollars for the purchase of the rights to the widow's valuable property?

7. What role did the working people of Manifest play in Jinx's scheme? What role did the children play?

8. Why did Jinx have to do chores for Mrs. Larkin?

9. In 1938, why did Abilene, Lettie, and Ruthanne sneak into the closed school?

Questions for Discussion:

1. What do you think might be in Miss Sadies's gardening shed? Why would she keep its contents a secret?

2. Why do you think Ned's letters were usually so cheerful and light, despite the grim experience of a soldier in the trenches? Why do you think Ned has "lost track of exactly what we're fighting for"?

3. What is the difference between the way a flu epidemic was handled in Manifest in 1918 and the way it would be handled in your community today?

Literary Devices:

I. *Symbolism*—A symbol in literature is a person, object, or event that represents an idea or a set of ideas. What do you think Little Eva's nesting dolls symbolize?

_____

_____

Miss Sadie's Divining Parlor; No-Man's Land; Hattie Mae's News Auxiliary; Pvt. Ned Gillen; One Short, One Long; Miss Sadie's Divining Parlor; The Manifest Herald; Pvt. Ned Gillen; Ode to the Rattler (cont.)

II. *Irony*—Irony refers to a twist of fate or a situation that turns out to be the opposite of what is expected. What is ironic about the people of Manifest going to the Baptist Church for Velma T's elixir?

_____

_____

_____

What is ironic about Ned's statement in his letter from the trenches to Jinx, "I can picture everyone [at home] having the best dog-robbin' time"?

_____

_____

Social Studies/Science Connection:

Go online to do some additional research to find out how influenza in 1918 affected people and how many suffered and died. Learn how it spread around the world and why it was so deadly. You can also learn about the way the epidemic hit Camp Devens, a military camp near Boston.

Word Study:

Many words in English have more than one meaning and act as different parts of speech. For example, this is true of the word "manifest":

- As an adjective, *manifest* means *obvious* or *apparent* as in *a manifest mistake*.

- As a verb, *manifest* means to *reveal* or *make known* as in *He manifested his delight with a hearty laugh*.

- As a noun, *manifest* means *a list of goods and people being transported by ship* as in *Every one of the immigrants traveling aboard the steamer was named in the ship's manifest*.

If all of the meanings of *manifest* have to do with <u>visibility</u> or <u>openness</u>, why did Abilene think that *"Manifest"* was the wrong name for this town?

_____

_____

_____

Miss Sadie's Divining Parlor; No-Man's Land; Hattie Mae's News Auxiliary; Pvt. Ned Gillen; One Short, One Long; Miss Sadie's Divining Parlor; The Manifest Herald; Pvt. Ned Gillen; Ode to the Rattler (cont.)

Cooperative Learning Activity: Prediction

Work with a group of your classmates to fill in the first two columns in the prediction chart below. Compare your responses with those of other groups in your class.

Question	Prediction	Actual Outcome
Who will Jinx turn out to be?		
How will Miss Sadies's stories shed light on Manifest's deepest secrets?		
Will Abilene be reunited with her father?		
How will Ned Gillen's story turn out?		
Will Abilene remain in Manifest?		
What will happen to the Widow Cane's property?		
Will the identity of "The Rattler" be revealed?		

Writing Activities:

1. The death of the Widow Cane set off an "explosion" that put a series of events in motion. Write about a time when one incident in your life created a cause-and-effect sequence of events. How were each of these events related?

2. Imagine that you are Jinx, and write a letter to Ned explaining what is happening in Manifest while he is away at war.

Drawing Straws; Miss Sadie's Divining Parlor; Distribution; Miss Sadie's Divining Parlor; Hattie Mae's News Auxiliary; Miss Sadie's Divining Parlor; Day of Reckoning

Vocabulary: Word analogies are equations in which the first pair of words has the same relationship as the second pair of words. For example: MISERABLE is to UNHAPPY as DISGUISE is to CONCEAL. Both pairs of words are synonyms. Choose the best word from the Word Box to complete each of the analogies below.

WORD BOX			
charade	infirmity	pungent	somber
distribute	preposterous	rankle	vigil

1. GLADNESS is to JOY as WEAKNESS is to _____.

2. SENSIBLE is to _____ as CAREFUL is to RASH.

3. PRAISE is to FLATTER as INSULT is to _____.

4. DECEPTION is to _____ as VOW is to LOYALTY.

5. RESCUE is to SAVE as WATCH is to _____.

6. GATHER is to _____ as SAVE is to WASTE.

7. _____ is to PEPPER as BLAND is to OATMEAL.

8. FRIGID is to SCORCHING as JOYOUS is to _____.

> Read to find out why Sheriff Dean goes after Jinx.

Questions:

1. Why did Mr. Cooper inform Abilene that his father, Hermann Keufer, had not been a spy during the war?

2. Why did Abilene visit the cemetery? Why was she relieved when she did not find the object of her visit?

3. Why did the townspeople flock to the abandoned mine shaft?

4. Why did Sheriff Dean's suspicions about Jinx increase?

5. Why did the men put a dead pig in a casket?

6. What did Shady mean when he told Jinx that there must be a "mole" in Manifest?

Drawing Straws; Miss Sadie's Divining Parlor; Distribution; Miss Sadie's Divining Parlor; Hattie Mae's News Auxiliary; Miss Sadie's Divining Parlor; Day of Reckoning (cont.)

7. How did the girls plan to trap the writer of the warning note that had been left on the tree?

8. How did Devlin and Burton get tricked into bidding for the parcel of water with the spring on it, rather than on the more valuable land with the vein of ore beneath it?

9. What enabled the townspeople to purchase the parcel of land containing the ore?

Questions for Discussion:

1. Why do you think a somber mood hung over the gathering at Shady's place? Why was Abilene's innocent remark met with silence and uneasiness?

2. What do you think might have happened to Margaret Evans to turn her mother into the "stone lady" that Abilene often noticed sitting on the front porch?

3. Do you think there was a mole in Manifest? If so, who might it be?

4. When Jinx complained that bad luck followed him around like a shadow, why did Shady suggest he outrun his shadow or stare it down? What would you do?

5. In his letter to Jinx of September 12, 1918, what did Ned suggest about his mood and that of the troops?

6. Do you think Devlin and Burton will accept their defeat or seek revenge?

Literary Devices:

I. *Foreshadowing*—Foreshadowing refers to the clues an author provides to suggest later events in the story. Why might Mrs. Dawkins warn Abilene against stirring up old memories of Manifest?

_____

_____

II. *Simile*—What is being compared in the following simile:

> There followed a most painful silence that hovered like hot, moist air before a big rain.

_____

Why is this better than just saying, "Everyone was silent"?

_____

_____

Drawing Straws; Miss Sadie's Divining Parlor; Distribution; Miss Sadie's Divining Parlor; Hattie Mae's News Auxiliary; Miss Sadie's Divining Parlor; Day of Reckoning (cont.)

III. *Personification*—What is being personified in the following passage:

> See how these letters are straight up and down, plodding across the page? And at the end of each word, the last letter trails off like it's giving out its dying breath.

_____

What does this image suggest about the writer of the note?

_____

_____

Social Studies Connection:

Do some research to learn about the Quakers in America. Why did they come to America? How do they observe their religion? What is characteristic of a Quaker meeting? Find out what Abilene meant when she "suddenly realized that the room had grown quiet with that kind of Quaker anticipation—waiting for the next Friend to speak."

Writing Activities:

1. Write about a real or imagined time when you suspected that someone was playing a trick on you. What were the circumstances? Did you confront this person? How did the situation turn out?

2. Write a "Remember When" story about an incident that occurred in your life. Try to give your story a beginning, a middle, and an end.

Hattie Mae's News Auxiliary; Pvt. Ned Gillen; The Jungle; Remember When; Miss Sadie's Divining Parlor; Homecoming; Miss Sadie's Divining Parlor; St. Dizier; Pvt. Ned Gillen; The Shadow of Death; The Shed; The Diviner; Beginnings, Middles, and Ends; The Rattler; Hattie Mae's News Auxiliary

Vocabulary: Antonyms are words with opposite meanings. Draw a line from each word in column A to its antonym in column B. Then use the words in column A to fill in the blanks in the sentences below.

A		B	
1.	humid	a.	end
2.	festers	b.	smooth
3.	perpetuate	c.	innocent
4.	vibrant	d.	disturbance
5.	degenerate	e.	neglected
6.	contorted	f.	dry
7.	consolation	g.	heals
8.	nurtured	h.	dull

. . . .

1. The lawyer insisted that his client shaved and dressed in good clothes so that he would not appear to be a(n) _____ before the judge and jury.

2. The child's face was _____ from anxiety and grief.

3. This _____ weather reminds me of a tropical jungle.

4. The troubling newspaper article about the war offered no _____ to its readers.

5. We _____ the tiny kittens who had no mother to tend to them.

6. I love the _____ colors of the garden in full bloom.

7. Waiting for bad news can only _____ the worry and concern one feels.

8. A wound that has not been cleaned sometimes _____.

> Read to find out whether Miss Sadie's stories solve all the mysteries of the town of Manifest.

Hattie Mae's News Auxiliary; Pvt. Ned Gillen; The Jungle; Remember When; Miss Sadie's Divining Parlor; Homecoming; Miss Sadie's Divining Parlor; St. Dizier; Pvt. Ned Gillen; The Shadow of Death; The Shed; The Diviner; Beginnings, Middles, and Ends; The Rattler; Hattie Mae's News Auxiliary (cont.)

Questions:

1. What did the mineworkers gain as a result of the auction and the judge's decision?

2. What important world news did Hattie Mae have for her readers in her news article of October 2, 1918?

3. What did Ned's letter of October 4, 1918, reveal about the dangers still facing the soldiers in Europe?

4. What did Abilene learn about Shady when she ventured one night into "The Jungle"? How did this change her theories about Shady?

5. How did the girls pinpoint the identity of The Rattler? Were they correct?

6. Why was Miss Sadie miserable and depressed when Abilene ran to tell her the news about the discovery of The Rattler's identity?

7. What did Shady mean when he said that they could "throw the sheriff a bone"?

8. Why did Sheriff Dean give up the chase when he saw Finn's body in the grave instead of Jinx's?

9. How did Jinx react to the death of his friend Ned?

10. Why did Shady take Abilene to a remote cemetery in Manifest? What did she learn from this experience?

11. Why had Miss Sadie allowed her son Ned to be raised by the Gillen family? What helped to ease the pain of separation for her?

12. Why was it particularly meaningful that Miss Sadie was invited by the women of the town to contribute the center square of the friendship quilt?

13. What brought Jinx, Abilene's father, back to Manifest after so many years?

14. Who was the shadowy figure that had been glimpsed in the woods in 1918? Why would this have been significant in the development of events in this story?

15. What evidence showed that Abilene chose to make Manifest her *home*?

Hattie Mae's News Auxiliary; Pvt. Ned Gillen; The Jungle; Remember When; Miss Sadie's Divining Parlor; Homecoming; Miss Sadie's Divining Parlor; St. Dizier; Pvt. Ned Gillen; The Shadow of Death; The Shed; The Diviner; Beginnings, Middles, and Ends; The Rattler; Hattie Mae's News Auxiliary (cont.)

Questions for Discussion:

1. Why do you think the German soldier spared Ned's life?

2. How did Ned's letters affect your attitude toward war?

3. Why do you think Shady spent his nights helping homeless people?

4. Why do you suppose Miss Sadie wouldn't let her wound be lanced until she had finished her last story?

5. Why do you think Miss Sadie had warned Abilene to stay away from the old shed? Why did it no longer matter if Abilene discovered its contents?

6. In what ways was Miss Sadie's pronouncement that "Things are not always what they seem" true in the town of Manifest?

7. How did Miss Sadie's words, "who would dream that one can love without being crushed under the weight of it," help Abilene understand her father and his need to send her to Manifest?

8. In what ways was story-telling therapeutic for the town of Manifest and the people who lived there? Do you think it is a good idea for people to tell their stories, including both the good and the bad?

Literary Device: Symbolism

What did the act of lancing Miss Sadie's wound symbolize?

_____

_____

_____

What did the compass that Abilene found in the box symbolize?

_____

_____

_____

Hattie Mae's News Auxiliary; Pvt. Ned Gillen; The Jungle; Remember When; Miss Sadie's Divining Parlor; Homecoming; Miss Sadie's Divining Parlor; St. Dizier; Pvt. Ned Gillen; The Shadow of Death; The Shed; The Diviner; Beginnings, Middles, and Ends; The Rattler; Hattie Mae's News Auxiliary (cont.)

Literary Element: Characterization

During the course of the novel, we learn a good deal about many of the residents of Manifest. How did your view of each of these characters change from the beginning until the end of the novel?

Character	Beginning	End
Abilene		
Shady		
Jinx		
Miss Sadie		
Sheriff Dean		
Eudora Larkin		
Ned Gillen		

Social Studies Connection:

1. Read the section on Immigrants in the Author's Note at the end of the book and do some additional research to learn about Ellis Island. In what years did it operate as an immigrants' gateway to America? Under what circumstances were immigrants denied entry? Then do some family research to find out whether any of your ancestors passed through Ellis Island.

2. Read about Orphan Trains in the Author's Note at the end of the book and do some additional research to learn about the orphan trains that brought orphans to live with families out west during the Depression. Find out when these train rides occurred. How were these orphans treated when they lived with their new families? Was this considered a successful experiment?

Hattie Mae's News Auxiliary; Pvt. Ned Gillen; The Jungle; Remember When; Miss Sadie's Divining Parlor; Homecoming; Miss Sadie's Divining Parlor; St. Dizier; Pvt. Ned Gillen; The Shadow of Death; The Shed; The Diviner; Beginnings, Middles, and Ends; The Rattler; Hattie Mae's News Auxiliary (cont.)

Writing Activities:

1. Did you ever tell a white lie to protect another person? What were the circumstances? Write a description of this event and its consequences.

2. Ned Gillen's death had a great impact on many of the people of Manifest. Based on what you learned about the character while reading the story, write an obituary, or brief biography, of Ned Gillen.

3. Imagine that you are Jinx. Write a journal entry expressing your thoughts and feelings on the day of Ned Gillen's funeral.

4. Imagine you are Abilene and write your first news column to replace "Hattie Mae's News Auxiliary." You may want to introduce yourself to those in the community who do not know you, tell how you came to Manifest, and suggest what you will write about in your column in the future.

CLOZE ACTIVITY

The following excerpt has been taken from the chapter "Sacred Heart of the Holy Redeemer Elementary School, May 28, 1936." Read it through completely. Then fill in each blank with a word that makes sense. Afterwards, you may compare your language with that of the author.

No matter. I'd have this _____¹ whipped into shape lickety-split. First off, I _____² out the straightest nail I could find _____³ fixed that sign right up. Fort Treeconderoga was _____⁴ for business.

Kneeling in front of one _____⁵ the crates like it was an altar, _____⁶ opened the cigar box and let the _____⁷ tumble out. There was the map. Not _____⁸ folded-up road map, but a homemade one _____⁹ faded paper with worn edges. It was _____¹⁰ hand-drawn picture of places around the town, _____¹¹ with names. Up top in a youthful _____¹² were the words *The Home Front*.

Then there were _____¹³ keepsakes. Little things kept for the sake _____¹⁴ something. Or someone. A cork, a fishhook, _____¹⁵ silver dollar, a fancy key, and a _____¹⁶ wooden baby doll, no bigger than a _____,¹⁷ painted in bright colors, with a face _____¹⁸ everything. To me they were like treasures _____¹⁹ a museum, things a person could study _____²⁰ learn about another time and the people _____²¹ lived back then.

Then there were the _____.²² I selected one and held the thin _____²³ to my nose, wondering, hoping that I'd _____²⁴ something of Gideon as a boy. Maybe _____²⁵ like dog, or wood, or pond water. _____²⁶ felt like I was floating in my _____²⁷ world of summer, and hide-and-seek, and fishing _____²⁸ I opened the paper and read the _____.²⁹ *Dear Jinx*, it said in an unfamiliar penmanship. _____³⁰ heart sank like a five-gallon bucket full _____³¹ disappointment. The cigar box and letters _____³² to Gideon. But I kept reading.

POST-READING ACTIVITIES AND QUESTIONS FOR DISCUSSION

1. Return to the chart of Plot Details for 1936 and 1918 that you began in the Pre-Reading Activities on page five of this study guide. Complete your list of major events for each time period. Compare your responses with those of others who have read the same book. Discuss how the two plot lines converge and enlighten each other.

2. Return to the Conflict chart that you began on page sixteen of this study guide. Add more information and then compare your responses with those of your classmates. Were all conflicts resolved at the end of the book? Did you find the resolutions to be satisfying? What conflicts remained unresolved?

3. **Pair/Share:** Work with a partner and return to the chart of predictions that you made on page twenty-three of this study guide. Discuss the actual outcome of each of your predictions and then write them in your chart. Compare your responses with those of other pairs.

4. Return to page nine of this study guide and make corrections and additions to the vernacular chart. Compare your responses with those of your classmates.

5. Why do you think the book was titled *Moon Over Manifest*? Why is the town itself so important to the novel? If you had to choose a new title for this book, what would it be?

6. Write a sequel to *Moon Over Manifest*, telling what happens to Abilene, Gideon, Shady and the other inhabitants of Manifest, Kansas.

7. Miss Sadie deals with unhappiness by shaping stories about the past, and Gideon tries to avoid pain by running from it. How do each of the other characters in the novel deal with sadness and loss?

8. Miss Sadie and Abilene both believe that the stories we tell and hear help us to understand the past. With a group of classmates, discuss why storytelling is an important human activity. What else may be gained by the telling of stories, both factual and fictional? How were stories told in the past? How are they told today?

9. **Music Connection:** Songs play a part in this novel. What are some song lyrics that are significant to you? Write down these lyrics or play recordings of songs for a group of classmates, then hold a discussion of how these songs create an emotional atmosphere.

10. **Literary Element: Theme**—A theme in a literary work is its controlling idea or message. *Moon Over Manifest* has several important themes. Consider the following themes and discuss how each is developed in the novel:
    - coming to terms with loss
    - overcoming stereotypes and snobbery
    - the power of the past over the present
    - the need for human companionship
    - the ties that form a community

Post-Reading Activities and Questions for Discussion (cont.)

11. The town of Manifest was rife with prejudice. What prejudices of race and class were evident? How did Miss Sadie and Abilene help the town address their prejudices? What examples of prejudice can you identify in your community? In what ways, if any, does your community address its prejudices?

12. Write about one part of your personal history that remains a secret from most of the people who know you. Keep this story hidden until you feel comfortable sharing it with another person. When you do share it, does the sharing make you feel better or worse? Would you advise others to share their stories?

13. **Art Connection/Story Summary:** Create a cigar box of mementos for *Moon Over Manifest*. Place inside an old cigar box or any other small box the following items: skeleton key, compass, Wiggle King fishing lure, silver dollar, cork, and Eva's nesting doll. You may use actual items or substitute pictures of the items mounted on card stock. Provide a short description of the item, tell why it was important in the book, and attach this to the item.

14. **Literature Circle:** Have a literature circle discussion in which you tell your personal reactions to *Moon Over Manifest*. Here are some questions to help your literature circle begin a discussion.

    • Do you identify with Abilene or Jinx in any way? Do you identify with any other character?

    • Did this book provide you with any new insights into the lives of people you would never have known otherwise?

    • Do you think the characters and the way they spoke were presented in a realistic fashion? Why or why not?

    • Which character did you admire the most? The least?

    • Who else would you like to read this novel? Why?

SUGGESTIONS FOR FURTHER READING

Fiction

Babbitt, Natalie. *The Eyes of the Amaryllis*. Farrar, Straus, Giroux.

* _____. *Tuck Everlasting*. Farrar, Straus, Giroux.

Byars, Betsy. *The Not-Just-Anybody Family*. Random House.

* _____. *The Pinballs*. Scholastic.

* Cormier, Robert. *I Am the Cheese*. Random House.

* Fitzhugh, Louise. *Harriet the Spy*. Random House.

Glaser, Diane. *The Diary of Trilby Frost*. Random House.

* Hamilton, Virginia. *M.C. Higgins, The Great*. Simon & Schuster.

* Hesse, Karen. *Out of the Dust*. Scholastic.

* Holt, Kimberly Willis. *When Zachary Beaver Came to Town*. Henry Holt.

* Hunt, Irene. *No Promises in the Wind*. Penguin.

Landis, J.D. *Daddy's Girl*. HarperCollins.

Lenski, Lois. *Strawberry Girl*. Random House.

* Lowry, Lois. *Anastasia Krupnik*. Random House.

* Nixon, Jean Lowery. *A Family Apart*. Random House.

* Paterson, Katherine. *The Great Gilly Hopkins*. HarperCollins.

* Peck, Richard. *A Long Way from Chicago*. Penguin.

Salassi, Otto. *And Nobody Knew They Were There*. HarperCollins.

* Smith, Doris Buchanan. *A Taste of Blackberries*. HarperCollins.

Townsend, John Rowe. *Dan Alone*. HarperCollins.

Yep, Laurence. *Star Fisher*. Penguin.

Nonfiction

Freedman, Russell. *Children of the Great Depression*. Houghton Mifflin Harcourt.

* NOVEL-TIES Study Guide are available for these titles.

ANSWER KEY

Santa Fe Railway; Hattie Mae's News Auxiliary; Path to Perdition; Shady's Place; First Morning; Sacred Heart of the Holy Redeemer Elementary School; Fort Treeconderoga; Main Street, Manifest; Miss Sadie's Divining Parlor

Vocabulary: 1. h 2. d 3. i 4. c 5. f 6. a 7. e 8. g 9. b; 1. receptive 2. antiquity 3. reluctant 4. sparse 5. perdition 6. dilapidated 7. lumbered 8. vigilant 9. predicament

Questions: 1. Abilene was traveling to a town she had never seen before because her father wanted her to visit his childhood home town for the summer. His alleged motivation for sending her away is that she needs to be cared for while he works a railroad job in another state. 2. When Abilene said, "I liked imagining that the chain of that broken compass was long enough to stretch all the way back into his pocket, with him at one end and me at the other," she meant that wherever she and her father were, she felt a strong connection with him. 3. Abilene jumped off the moving train because she wanted to survey Manifest before its inhabitants observed her. 4. When Abilene first met Pastor Howard, she didn't think he looked, spoke, or acted like a clergyman, and that his home was an odd conglomeration of saloon, church, and rundown home; she was surprised by the dilapidation of the building and unsettled by the adjacent cemetery. 5. Abilene did not think the town of Manifest looked like the town described by her father. In its dilapidated state, it was neither "smooth" nor "sweet" and no one in town was bustling. The Depression had forced the closing of many stores and businesses in Manifest and given its residents a tired, dispirited attitude. 6. From reading old newspapers and poking around Shady's living quarters, Abilene hoped to discover more about her father's early years and about the history of the town. 7. Abilene thought it was luxurious to have water for washing available without going to the pump; she thought she was in a fancy hotel when a meal was cooked for her. She felt this way because before coming to Manifest, Abilene had been living a hard and transient life on the railroads with her father. 8. By the term "universals," Abilene meant people and situations that were so common, that they seemed immediately familiar. 9. At first, Abilene was rude to Lettie and Ruthanne when they visited her at the tree house because she thought they had come as an act of charity, and she resented this. 10. The girls were frightened by the note because they assumed that it had been left there by The Rattler, the presumed spy of the World War II years whom Abilene had read about in the hidden papers. They were also scared because The Rattler knew they were looking for him. 11. Abilene visited Miss Sadie's home because she saw her lost compass hanging on the porch. Too frightened to retrieve it that night, she returned in daylight, hoping Miss Sadie would let her have it.

Triple Toe Creek; A Bargain is Struck; Likely Suspects; Hattie Mae's News Auxiliary; Miss Sadie's Divining Parlor; The Art of Distraction; Frog Hunting; Miss Sadie's Divining Parlor

Vocabulary: 1. h 2. e 3. a 4. i 5. b 6. g 7. c 8. d 9. f; 1. saunter 2. pathetic 3. intrigued 4. restitution 5. touted 6. rile 7. convivial 8. jubilant 9. concoction

Questions: 1. Jinx tricked Ned by trading him a smelly potion for a fish for supper, claiming the mixture was a refreshing tonic that would attract the girl he loved. 2. Arthur Devlin had power over the people of Manifest because he owned the local coal mine and the company store, where people were forced to make their purchases with vouchers for their wages instead of cash. 3. The Ku Klux Klan members gathered by Triple Toe Creek in order to plan an attack on innocent immigrants; Jinx and Ned foiled their plans by substituting poison ivy leaves for newspaper in the outhouse. 4. Miss Sadie said she was a diviner rather than a fortune teller because she did not predict the future, but closely examined things that most people failed to notice: this allowed her to understand the true meaning of puzzling situations. 5. Abilene agreed to do odd jobs for Miss Sadie in return for breaking a precious pot; it was the only way she could get her compass back from Miss Sadie. 6. The mementos and papers in the cigar box convinced Abilene that there was truth to Miss Sadie's stories of the past. 7. Jinx lived with Shady when he came to Manifest. 8. Burton compelled Ned to work a double shift at the mine by threatening to demand immediate payment of a debt, the unpaid balance the Gillens family owed to the company store. 9. Jinx "borrowed" the Manchurian Fire Thrower because he wanted to reproduce it and go into the firecracker business with Ned. Answers to the second part of the question will vary. 10. Abilene was distracted from further investigation of the grave marker by the unexpected sight of Sister Redempta out of her nun's habit, tending to a woman who was giving birth.

The Victory Quilt; Pvt. Ned Gillen; Under the Stars; Pvt. Ned Gillen; Hattie Mae's News Auxiliary

Vocabulary: 1. f 2. d 3. g 4. e 5. h 6. b 7. a 8. c

Questions: 1. The women of Manifest were making a Victory Quilt to auction off in support of the armed forces fighting the world war. 2. Mrs. Larkin refused to associate with Miss Sadie and discouraged her daughter from associating with Ned Gillen because she, as a member of the DAR, considered herself and her daughter to be in a class above those of more recent American ancestry. 3. Lance Devlin was furious that the son of one of his father's employees at the mine, someone who he believed was his social inferior, could beat him in competitive races. 4. After Jinx was orphaned and went to live with his Uncle Finn, he was made his assistant: he learned all of the cons that his uncle perpetrated successfully at missions and tent revivals. Jinx used this knowledge to start his firecracker business and to win games of chance at the New Year's festivities. 5. As revealed in a flashback from 1917, Jinx was present when his uncle had killed a man. Jinx left his uncle, went on the run to escape him and the life he offered, and he needed to stay clear of law enforcement officials who might accuse him of the murder. 6. Ned was able to use the money he had gotten from his half of the firecracker sales to enlist. The recruiting officer was so distracted by the festivities and by the twenty-five dollar bribe that he didn't bother to confirm Ned's age. Ned wanted to serve in the army to show off his courage and patriotism and to escape the narrow-mindedness of Manifest. 7. Shady demanded that Jinx bid high on the Victory Quilt as punishment for selling firecrackers and for the water tower explosion; he had to use all the money he earned at his illicit endeavors to pay for the quilt. 8. It was clear that the three girls were superstitious when they all feared the return of the ghost in the story they just told as they were walking in the woods. They were also searching for the Rattler, a shadowy spy from the past.

Miss Sadie's Divining Parlor; Elixir of Life; Hattie Mae's News Auxiliary; Dead or Alive

Vocabulary: 1. d 2. b 3. e 4. h 5. c 6. a 7. f 8. g; 1. peer 2. fugitive 3. refuge 4. mingled 5. abolish 6. demise 7. scheme 8. evade

Questions: 1. Sheriff Dean had the advantage of the law over Shady, who was manufacturing illegal alcoholic beverages during Prohibition; he used his power to get free drink and other items from Shady. 2. Shady protected Jinx from the Sheriff because he believed that Jinx was innocent of any serious wrongdoing. When he told Jinx that he suspected that he was in the wrong place at the wrong time, he meant that the boy was not the instigator or the perpetrator of the crime, but just happened to be on the scene when a crime was committed. 3. The burning wooden cross had been placed in front of the German Fraternal Hall by the Ku Klux Klan, the members of which had the double purpose of trying to stop them from organizing a union of coal miners, and threatening them because the United States was at war with Germany. 4. To save Shady from the Sheriff's anger at not being given his full quota of illegal liquor, Jinx substituted Velma T's elixir for the alcohol, which would not be ready on time. 5. Abilene was frustrated in her search to find information about her father because no one, not even Shady, was willing to talk about him. 6. Abilene was collecting plants for Miss Sadie's potions as a way to work off her punishment for breaking her Hungarian pot.

Miss Sadie's Divining Parlor; No-Man's Land; Hattie Mae's News Auxiliary; Pvt. Ned Gillen; One Short, One Long; Miss Sadie's Divining Parlor; The Manifest Herald; Pvt. Ned Gillen; Ode to the Rattler

Vocabulary: 1. fortunate–the other words are alike because they all mean cheerless 2. openly–the other words are alike because they all mean slyly 3. supporting–the other words are alike because they all refer to a way of manipulating someone or something 4. worried–the other words are alike because they all mean excited or enlivened 5. release–the other words are alike because they all refer to a blockage or standoff 6. explanation–the other words are alike because they all refer to deception 7. dissuade–the other words are alike because they all mean to influence by persuasion 8. credible–the other words are alike because they all suggest something is so odd to provoke fear

Questions: 1. Abilene continued to work for Miss Sadie because she needed to hear more stories of Manifest in order to piece together the full history of the town and its impact on her father. 2. Arthur Devlin knew there was ore buried beneath the widow's property, and he wanted to get his hands on it. 3. Miss Velma's elixir suddenly became popular because it was spiked with alcohol by Shady and Jinx and it became readily available. 4. Miss Sadie's words reminded the people that they all shared the immigrant experience and that their families had made great sacrifices so that they might come to America and gain freedom and prosperity. 5. The town of Manifest was put on quarantine so that the influenza epidemic wouldn't spread beyond the town. In this era before antibiotics, this was the only public health option available. 6. Jinx planned to feign a flu epidemic in Manifest so as to scare off the well-to-do who could afford a vacation, and meanwhile raise the money by manufacturing large quantities of corn whiskey. 7. The working people of Manifest pretended to be flu sufferers in order to scare off their enemies; the children played the role of sentries, watching to see that no intruders entered the town. 8. Jinx had to do chores for Mrs. Larkin so that she would not prosecute him for selling the illegal moonshine. 9. Abilene, Lettie, and Ruthanne snuck into the closed school in search of Stucky Cybulskis' "Ode to the Rattler."

Drawing Straws; Miss Sadie's Divining Parlor; Distribution; Miss Sadie's Divining Parlor; Hattie Mae's News Auxiliary; Miss Sadie's Divining Parlor; Day of Reckoning

Vocabulary: 1. infirmity 2. preposterous 3. rankle 4. charade 5. vigil 6. distribute 7. pungent 8. somber

Questions: 1. Mr. Cooper, worried about what Abilene would discover in her search for the Rattler, informed Abilene that his father, Hermann Keufer, had not been a spy during the war: any suggestion to the contrary was just a result of the widespread prejudice against people of German extraction during the war. 2. Abilene visited the cemetery, hoping to get information about Mrs. Evans's deceased daughter from the headstone. Abilene was relieved when she didn't find the headstone because it restored her hope that Margaret Evans might still be alive. 3. The townspeople flocked to the abandoned mine shaft to buy Miss Velma's new, improved concoction, which was known to fight off the symptoms of the flu and speed the recovery process. 4. The sighting of a man who fit the description of one of the fugitives, a man who had come briefly to the mine shaft and had seen Jinx, made Sheriff Dean still more suspicious that Jinx was one of the two fugitives. 5. The men put a dead pig in a casket to deter Lester Burton from checking further on the miners' activities, thus buying a little more time for Shady and Jinx to raise the thousand dollars to buy the Widow Cane's property. The pig in the casket was supposed to be the corpse of an influenza victim. 6. When Shady told Jinx that there must be a mole in Manifest, he was referring to a possible informant leaking information about the whiskey concoction to Devlin and his cohorts. 7. The girls planned to trap the writer of the note by getting Miss Hattie to hold a writing contest, so that they could compare handwriting samples to the writing on the note. 8. Jinx, along with Eudora Larkin, who had been offended by Devlin's cavalier advances to her and snide attitude about her late husband, had conspired to pass off Eudora's son-in-law as a government inspector impressed by the healthy properties of the spring water. 9. The townspeople were able to purchase the parcel of land containing the ore because Devlin, by buying the land with the "health promoting spring water," had to pay the town back taxes due on that property. This provided the townspeople of Manifest the funds to purchase the parcel of land with the ore.

Hattie Mae's News Auxiliary; Pvt. Ned Gillen; The Jungle; Remember When; Miss Sadie's Divining Parlor; Homecoming; Miss Sadie's Divining Parlor; St. Dizier; Pvt. Ned Gillen; The Shadow of Death; The Shed; The Diviner; Beginnings, Middles, and Ends; The Rattler; Hattie Mae's News Auxiliary

Vocabulary: 1. f 2. g 3. a 4. h 5. c 6. b 7. d 8. e; 1. degenerate 2. contorted 3. humid 4. consolation 5. nurtured 6. vibrant 7. perpetuate 8. festers

Questions: 1. In exchange for access to the underground ore on the land now owned by the town of Manifest, the mine workers gained the right to negotiate with Devlin about new working codes and payment. 2. Hattie Mae was able to inform her readers that there was news of a possible armistice and an end to the war in Europe. 3. Ned's letter revealed that apart from the constant risk of death in battle, soldiers were faced with the threat of dysentery, influenza, and death from exposure and sheer exhaustion. 4. When Abilene ventured into "The Jungle," she learned that Shady spent many of his nights at a hobo camp, serving coffee and food to the homeless; she no longer theorized that Shady went out drinking at night. 5. The girls discovered the identity of The Rattler by matching the writing samples from the contest entries with the writing on the paper that had been posted on the tree; the Rattler turned out to be Mr. Underhill. They were partly correct: he had spied on the townspeople when they were planning to trick Devlin, but he wasn't a spy for the enemy. 6. Miss Sadie was depressed because her leg was not healing and because the optimism of the people in Manifest in 1918 hadn't been founded on reality. 7. When Shady said to "throw a bone" to the Sheriff, he meant they should offer him just enough information to distract him from tracking Jinx. 8. Sheriff Dean gave up the chase when he saw Finn's body instead of Jinx's because he reasoned that with the more seriously guilty party dead, justice had been done: furthermore, this was a way of snubbing Sheriff Nagleman. 9. Jinx reacted to Ned's death by running away from Manifest, believing that he was guilty of his friend's death because he had helped him to raise the money to bribe the recruitment officer. 10. Shady took Abilene to the remote cemetery upon her request. Abilene learned that every family in Manifest was badly affected by the second influenza epidemic that hit Manifest in 1918. 11. Miss Sadie had allowed the Gillen family to raise her son because she believed he would be happier and better adjusted with them as opposed to living with her, a gypsy woman who would be shunned by the town. Having Sister Redempta show her Ned's report cards and other information helped her to feel that she was still connected to him. 12. When Miss Sadie was invited by the women of the town to contribute the center square of the friendship quilt, it served as an apology to her by the women of Manifest who had scorned her as an immigrant and an outsider in 1918. 13. Abilene's telegram to her father, indicating that she was ill and close to death, brought him back to town. 14. The shadowy figure that had been glimpsed in the woods in 1918 was most likely Sister Redempta; this would have been significant because her approach had resulted in the injury to Finn that prevented him from exposing or killing Jinx. 15. It was clear that Abilene had chosen Manifest as her home when Hattie Mae indicated in her column that Abilene would be her immediate successor as a local newspaper reporter.